PIRENE'S FOUNTAIN

PIRENE'S FOUNTAIN

VOLUME 14, ISSUE 22

Pirene's Fountain: A Journal of Poetry
Volume 14, Issue 22
Copyright © 2021 Pirene's Fountain
Paperback ISSN 2331-1096

Editor: Megan Merchant
Layout, Book & Cover Design: Steven Asmussen
Cover Artist: © Martin Lehmann | Dreamstime.com

All rights reserved: except for the purpose of quoting brief passages for review, no part of this book may be reproduced or transmitted in any form or by any means, electronic or mechanical, including photocopying, recording, or by any information storage and retrieval system, without permission in writing from the publisher.

Glass Lyre Press, LLC
P.O. Box 2693
Glenview, IL 60025

www.GlassLyrePress.com

CONTENTS

Poetry

Jeff Alfier
Farmer's Tale — Big Horn County   9

Clara Burghelea
Ars Amandi (or how to remember the homeland)   10
Portrait of My Mother in the Middle of Things   11

David Capps
Poem after Práxilla   12

Roxana Cazan
Bread Making   13
Pantoum with Dying and Giving Birth   15

Jaewon Chang
Mnemophobia   16
Ganggangsullae   17

Karen Douglass
"Christina's World"   18

Joyce Futa
Small Days   19

Shanta Gander
Curatorial Tags for the Exhibition: What Home Means When People, Places, and Things Go Missing Between Wake and Sleep   20

Marina Kazakova
From Upper Manhattan Down series 1 & 2   23

Kate LaDew
Spike Hughes, Britain's earliest jazz composer, said, sooner or later   27

Rustin Larson
The Pennsylvania   30

Joseph Mills
Ever After   32

Michael Minassian
To Say Goodbye   33
Nine Times Out Of Ten   34

Cameron Morse
    Seldom Is   35

Tayve Neese
    In spring, my denial still will not thaw   36
    We are all Crusoe in the slant light   37

Connie Post
    The Lie   38

Rose M. Smith
    Learning Classes   40

Crystal Stone
    Last Iowa Caucus   41
    My Phone: A Tombstone Memorializing   42

Sharon Tracey
    Derek Drove the John Deere Tractor   43
    After the Wildfire   44

Laura Van Prooyen
    Rupture   45
    Around the Block   46

Reviews

Unfinished Murder Ballads by Darren Demaree   49
The Unexploded Ordnance Bin by Rebecca Foust   53
The Taste of Earth by Hedy Habra   57
Frances of the Wider Field by Laura Van Prooyen   62
A Piece of Peace: Everyday Mindfulness to Improve your Well-Being and Creativity by Sweta Vikram   65

Prompts

Contributor Notes

POETRY

Farmer's Tale — Big Horn County

Jeff Alfier

Winter's a grim exposé. He plods numb hours.
    Fields gray to vanishing points.

Wind resurrects the storm fall. He starts his diesels
    just to groan them awake, checks herds for frostbite.

Only the river, far behind him now, bears a sheen.
    On his cell to his wife,

his voice rattles like tumblers in a lock.
    At the edge of hearing, snow muffles a siren.

Dusk now, and the moon — harbored in overcast
    above an attic window, is a streetlight in a dream.

His daughter, awaiting her first date,
    drags a hand-me-down brush wildly through her hair.

Ars Amandi (or how to remember the homeland)

Clara Burghelea

antiseptic / burnt matches / fresh paint /

Black Sea algae / scratch of light /

mother's urine / two molars / polenta /

Arsène Lupin / thief gentleman /

rough thumb / wiping lipstick from teeth /

the intimacy of a fist / three-legged dog /

half-bread / on ration card / bruised knees /

backroom loom / macramé shoes /

the quiet hours of yarn / fresh wood /

shame slack in the mouth / shaving foam /

powdered milk / Penicillin shot /

foreign hand / brushing thigh / hairballs /

scream muscles / body of sags / chamomile tea /

catching dewdrops / fresh cow dung / resin /

knitting hands / unripe bananas / love on loan /

Persian rug fringes / nail polish remover /

stale snow / garlic braids / two-day beard /

all this came slow /

Portrait of My Mother in the Middle of Things

Clara Burghelea

The way she relished in sitting with daily life,
peeling potatoes for hours in a row, then doing
her nails burgundy red. *Forgetting is essential,*
she said as she dunked her fingers into hot water
only to emerge them perfectly polished, no smudge
whatsoever. She then flaked garlic cloves, sheer
skins piling up under her humming touch. She would
get a stamp on things—laundry, dishes, number of hugs,
night shifts, cigarette smoking, morning snuggles, and
everything by twos. Children, painkillers, bruises, shopping
bags, don't sees and cant's, dream skins shed down the cold
tiles, crocheting needles, blood-spoored pies, yesterdays
and tomorrows twinned in always. Wound loving its hurt.

Poem after Práxilla

David Capps

I have watched men rest beneath the gazebo.
I have watched them hit golf balls by the dozen
as thunderclouds gathered in the sky,
and the grass, fresh-cut, smelled of lemonade,
and the blue sky, five-minutes ago traversed
by white wisps of clouds cutting through
on their way to some foreign land, lie dreaming.
I have seen fan blades of the motel fan fly
in desperate ellipses, as if the park were beckoning,
and the birds, and the violin player beneath
its dying branches. I have lost my breath
before the golden choir whose song pierced though
the walls, painting corner to corner my room
with faint exhalations, as if everything essential
were brought to bear there: time, memory, work,
ripe cucumbers spilling out of a picnic basket
tipped open on the lawn, the bridesmaid who
gathered them like nothing happened, how her
hands cut sideways into the clear sky, interrupting
its crude sleep, startling the doves the bride
released from her cedar box, one after the next.

Bread Making

Roxana Cazan

I walk into the morning,
light spilling across the floor through
the bay window—this granular silence of God—

and tiptoe into the kitchen to marvel
at the raised dough, folded into pan,
swaddled like an infant.

I am multiple beings splitting inside me,
always hard to tether to the shore of a single
body, and I touch this dough,

the world barely holding us,
my star still hung up high but waiting
any minute to fall and break my back.

I touch the dough with one finger,
the touch is plump, and I feel my pulse
throbbing, my hands spread open,

my mother's, my grandmother's hands caressing
the dough, folding it tight like flesh,
knowing that we are tied to the race

against time, I thaw into the memory
of bread making, that crisp morning
when the Russians took down the door and the village.

My grandmother, only a girl,
(her hands tired from kneading, her walnut
braids specked with flour,)

shoved by a stronger arm into the side
of the well wall, ordered to wash clothes
in a language that copied her rolling R's,

ordered to stay/stop, caught in the barn,
sweating the way a calf does,
terrified of the blade's glint.

When a child is born, we welcome it
with bread and salt, and when a man dies,
we skip the salt, sprinkle it over the grave,

the crystals' seal a testament, a trench,
a trough that cups the weeping,
and traps all this remembering,

and in my kitchen, my dough is risen and ready,
and I am open and made and mother.

Pantoum with Dying and Giving Birth

Roxana Cazan

Of course we knew that this was going to happen / or at least
we imagined it would / that we would one day close her eyes /
with the tips of our fingers / and the summer air would feel /
hazy and honeyed / despite the stillness / or perhaps because of it /

but we close her eyes one day / with the tips of our fingers /
as if we are picking chickpeas / sifting through the stems and pods /
in the honey-hazed summer / the air crushed into silence /
the baby in my belly hungry and screaming / sliding over my bones /

like she does into this dying / dry as chickpea stems and pods /
wilted by her stunted dreams / the one about being locked inside
the house / during an air raid / when she was just a baby / swimming towards
the light / hungry inside those damned four walls / and screaming when

the bombs dropped / just down the street / while she was locked inside /
waiting to be delivered / to her mother / almost dead with fear /
inside those damned four walls / and screaming to be let out /
and now she lies here silent / sliding into death / while my son yearns /

to be let out /

Mnemophobia

Jaewon Chang

Imagine a cottage in Pagudpud farm
under red clouds, stories of bombs
trimmed down to green water reeds
and blank fields, like how
your dead family exists for
a single frame in a kaleidoscope.
When the walls are no longer upright,
a boy cuts the ground with twigs and
draws a house, a room, and his name.
Don't be scared, the loud sound
before silence is only a promise
to not forget your name. Family
is only family if you remember.

GANGGANGSULLAE

JAEWON CHANG

Under the white sky,
mugunghwa petals carve a path
to cornfields, seeds blanched atop soil,
the rain rushing in to erase.
A group of women in a circle, twirls,
as if their whittled scars
can be cured by blind apparitions.
Feet shuffle clockwise, wishing
history would dissipate with time, because
the province of Jeolla is no longer where they last saw it.
Their hanbok billows upon the congelation of labor,
bombed houses now houses of soil.
The swinging of their arms like pendulums,
arranged in curvilinear paths, an answer
to the ignited fields, brimming
with men wearing red uniforms.
When the sky reddens, under it,
they festoon faces, ones hopeful
for the next harvest.

"Christina's World"

Karen Douglass
Andrew Wyeth, 1948

A woman alone
lying in a field,
her back to us, her arms
skeletal, legs thin
at the hem of her pink dress.

She leans uphill
toward a house, weathered,
closed, gray, sharp-edged,
abandoned. Woman,

get up, climb the long hill.
She cannot stand.
I would have her turn,
face us and say, "I am the one
bright moment in this world."

SMALL DAYS

JOYCE FUTA

Each morning I make a list
of forgettable things to do:
cut the cantaloupe,
wash the shower curtain,
inventory my canned goods.

When evening comes
I am glad that another small day
is over. Somehow, I have filled it.

I can't say I'm depressed
or happy,
can't say I'm suffering,
as so many people are.

I've become the queen
of bread and honey
and a beggar picking
through old clothes.

Sometimes when I hear
a joyous wren
or YoYo Ma's cello,
I am reminded of a rich life.

But mostly I live in the dream
of my house, walking from room
to room, trying to find myself.

Curatorial Tags for the Exhibition: What Home Means When People, Places, and Things Go Missing Between Wake and Sleep

Shanta Gander

I. *Harold Street* (c.1988)
Harold Street, the childhood home
for a hot sec, the hot sec before
getting out. Something about a
guy about the house. The first
time I learn houses—like people—
can go missing.

II. *Index of Items and People Lost* (I) (c.1988)
Erase a grandmother, aunts, cousins
from the second and third floors. Pack
roller skates, the brass beds, Vietnam
photo albums, Dr. Seuss, Beatrix Potter,
alongside wedding photos, the bubble
gum pink robe, the first gun ever held
by my six-year-old hands.

III. *Index of Items and People Lost* (II) (c.1988)
And the Cabbage Patch Kids—Christie,
Lola, and Spencer. Pack with no ex-
planation. Doing what they say makes
everything easier. Memory teaches
code breaking training—the tongue in
questions that become taste buds
never exposed to air.

IV. *A Week of Unexplained Family Time at
Howard Johnson's* (c.1988)
Howard Johnson wasn't a family
vacation, yet we had all our stuff.
*Where does all the clothing go with
no bureau?* Their creamers soothing to
the tongue of one who doesn't know…

V. *Index of Items and People Lost* (III)
(c.1988)
The Black-Eyed Peas, the clown cup
once filled with grandma's banana
pudding, the hamster, the fish, the
record player, "Boogie Wonderland,"
Model Market, Mr. Thomas's store,
all taking up residence in that place, a
place no longer.

VI. *Untitled* (c.1988-89)
Howard Johnson's became the hotel
on the pike. Birth of the glow of the
television screen that spoke soothing.
The smell that trained my nose and
spirit to avoid the vernacular of poverty.

VII. *Index of Items and People Lost* (IV)
(c. 1988-89)
Hotels traded for Wanda's one room. The
place made awesome cause Church's
Chicken is across the street. Wanda-Mama's-
childhood-friend-reuse-the-bathtub-water
Wanda. Wanda's, where more things
gone missing like daddy's pants, like the

VIII. *Index of Items and People Lost* (V)
(c.1989 – 90)
one car that carries all our stuff. Something
about a mickey in a drink, something about
a room, a woman …Wanda's exchanged for
Auntie and Uncle's basement eventually
traded for our own place. The apartment
at 280 Collins Street.

VIV. *Index of Items and People Lost/New
Items for New Home* (VI)
(c.1989 – 90)
Me, mine, own quietly went missing
while no one ever says what any of this
is or was. I become a pedagogical expert
in *if it isn't named, if it isn't spoken,
then it didn't really happen*; A
cartographer of silences, the lost,
white spaces, the abandoned, stolen,
and forgotten.

X. *Untitled* (c.1990)
Speaking detachment becomes
no movement, no fad, but a
forced native tongue involving
a monastic life—holding vigil
and caretaking the reliquary
for all things gone missing.

From Upper Manhattan Down series 1 & 2

Marina Kazakova

1
From upper Manhattan down:
walls of buildings and walls of mankind,
walls in moving pictures and walls of moving bodies,
fir trees at corner shops,
fir trees on the shoulders of locals,
people with four or five dogs,
people with coffees-to-go,
coffees and people, big or small—all not strong enough
to make someone be able to climb over
New York 2019,
to make someone remember
the redbrick building
of Chelsea Hotel
where Patti Smith and Robert Mapplethorpe
once lived.
The building stands still and blurs in one's unbelieving eye.
An escape to Whitney's museum -
into the city of a hundred years ago -
a city by Man Ray,
the world of O'Keeffe's
breasts and hips of flowers,

of Jacob Lawrence's shouting hands,
of Maya Deren's dance for the camera,
of Diego Riviera's women in calla lilies,
of Beatrice Wood's "Embracing Couple"—
a couple of steps closer to the charcoal portrait
and you are finally
over Manhattan's walls,
embracing things tangible and intangible.

2
Adieu, New York.
Goodbye, East Village.
Was a delight to breathe
the 14th Street.
The first bookshop
I entered
had a Patti Smith book
signed -
a hundred bucks.
I photographed her autograph ,
and kept flying—
towards St. Mark's,
arrived minutes after
a mass.
People were coffees.

People were laughing.

People were grand pianos.

Tompkins Square Park:

I stood and listened to the squirrel's concentration

accompanied by a guitar

of an unknown singer/songwriter.

The Parkside Lounge:

Poets from the Big Apple and not.

I have recited to all and to the one

sitting to the right—

a flower among the poets,

a flower in my desert,

a flower in this winter.

Cafe MagAdor.

Here,

I tried to understand a lot:

contemporary art,

the syndrome of God,

the kindness,

the power.

Adieu, New York

I understood a fair amount—

I adore you—

even though

you seem to be too brutal -

most probably,

I'm wrong

because

Esse quam videri -

Cicero -

you are New York,

you're still too new,

too young,

much further

than me

with my heavy, but pleasant luggage—

my Russia.

Spike Hughes, Britain's earliest jazz composer, said, sooner or later

Kate LaDew

all thrushes sing the tune of the first movement of Mozart's
    symphony no. 40 in g minor
with a dead-on tempo and no mistakes,
a thought better and brighter than monkeys thrashing a
    typewriter
for an infinite amount of time until, almost surely,
    Shakespeare's complete works tumble out,
just a jumble of letters and punctuation and blank spaces to a
    monkey,
whereas a thrush or any songbird knows it's making music
using a special organ only they possess, the syrinx at the top of
    the windpipe,
each breath vibrating membranes inside and sending notes
    back out,
singing despite the risks, acting as a dinner bell for predators,
    an expensive use of energy
in a tiny little body held up by tiny little bones,
but a bird's heart is 4 percent of its weight
ruffling the downy feathers of its chest with every beat,
in a tenth of a second sweeping through more notes than a
    piano has keys
learning their songs while still in the nest by listening to the
    voices of their parents
their voice box - a vibrating sound source - sending air
    molecules bumping into each other,
creating a cascade of movement, a pressure wave
that enters our and every other creature's ears in a torrent of
    beauty,
including Mozart's, who kept a starling as a pet,
teaching the bird to sing his piano concertos,
constantly disappointed, as it was always sharp, but listening

    just the same
just like one night at the home of Baron van Swieten—a patron of
    the arts
whom Beethoven dedicated his first symphony to—
Mozart listened to his own Symphony No. 40,
one of only two he wrote in a minor key,
legs splayed, sunk low into a straight back chair,
=Baron van Swieten to his left, his wife Constanze to his right—
who, despite marrying again after his death, would be buried under
    a tombstone
with the inscription "Mozart's widow"—
it began darkly, the first of four movements played by the lower
    strings with divided violas,
a work of passion, of violence and grief, stealing so much of him in
    the creation,
the execution could never measure up, and, a moment into the
    second movement,
Mozart leapt to his feet, threw his chair back and left the room
now, hundreds of years later, if you go through the main entrance of
    the St. Marx Cemetery
in Vienna's third district, walk down an aisle of trees until they fork
    and look left
there's a plot, No. 179, with a large stone slab and an angel and a
    column
and grass and flowers and hand-written notes—
the spot restored in the 1950's after Germany's bombs left little
    scars in all the tombstones—
where, under the earth, Mozart is supposed to be,
and maybe he is, maybe, unlike all the other graves in St. Marx
    during the 18th century
he was not dug up after ten years, moved to make room for another
    body,
maybe they left Mozart right there,
but, either way, if Hughes is right, one day there was, or some day
    will be, a thrush
flying over wherever the bones that housed Mozart's imagination

    lie,
singing its colossal heart out,
to the tune of the first movement of his Symphony No. 40 in g
    minor
with a dead-on tempo and no mistakes

The Pennsylvania

Rustin Larson

Today I think of Mark Twain,
or Sam Clemens as he was known,
as a young man learning
to navigate the big river.

There is something tragic about
his brother that I can't quite
recall. This was before Sam began
to write. The air smelled big.

He could smell Keokuk from
where he stood in the pilot's
box. It smelled like enormous
green frogs. In the pilot's

box of the east room, I can
watch the sun rise and the children
walk to school. I steer my house
around the eddies of another year.

I'd clang a bell if there was one.
Even so, I have only one brother left
alive. We do not communicate.
Pigeons whirl around the high school.

Twain's brother, he was not born in
an icebox. I remember now. Henry Clemens
died when the SS Pennsylvania exploded,
a riverboat Sam quit only weeks before.

EVER AFTER

JOSEPH MILLS

There aren't many photos of the after-prom party.
Plenty were taken before, when we were still brushed
and tucked, but afterwards, we were too busy drinking
and pulling one another into dark rooms to bother
with cameras. There are a few candids, dimly lit or
washed out in flash, blurred motion, red eyes, skin,
all of it still smooth. Even when a face is in focus,
I no longer know who it is, and I might not have then.
There is one photo of a boy half-naked, passed out,
something scrawled in black marker on his forehead.
Potato chips and beer cans are stacked on his body.
At the time, this would have been hilarious; now,
having teenagers of my own, it isn't as funny.
I remember at some point, he began puking,
and since we knew about Bon Scott, Bonham, Hendrix,
the dangers of choking to death on your vomit,
we rolled him onto his side, feeling adult at this
show of responsibility, and we continued partying.
Then, a girl appeared, someone I had known for years
but never talked to. She had a mop, bucket and rags,
somehow she had known where to get them. She knelt
in her dress and cleaned up the mess with an efficiency
that even then, drunk and at the apex of my jackass years,
I found remarkable. I don't remember the prom theme,
where it was held, who I took, or why I asked them;
I do remember this woman who knew what work was
and who did it because she knew it needed to be done.

To Say Goodbye

Michael Minassian

She must have known
how it would end—
dust along the shelves,
faded chenille spreads,
empty hangers,
and a forgotten brush
with a chipped handle
and strands of gray hair
as if they were made
of paper rolled
into a tight fist.

Nine Times Out Of Ten

Michael Minassian

Nine times out of ten,
one photograph is missing,
a piece of the puzzle lost
like a kissing cousin gone bad.

Along the last road in the county,
a catfish flops in a puddle far from any lake
like a forgotten phone call on an old-time
party line a neighbor forgot to hang up.

I had a pair of shoes once
I wore every day of summer
until my friend Billy drowned
in the Oradell reservoir,
and I couldn't bear to see his name
scrawled alongside the others
on the back of the black & white Keds—
the same ones I had on when I watched
his body brought to shore—
his bare feet swollen and pale
as two loaves of wet bread.

So I took those shoes and threw
them up on the telephone wires
outside the high school gym—
some say you could hear
his name being whispered
every time the phone rang
in that hollow space between hello
and another voice answering back.

Seldom Is

Cameron Morse

Light slides along threads of spider web
loosened from last night's black
hoodie. That's God
fingering the strings, I guess, being pious
for once. Lili leaves me
alone Sunday morning to sulk in the empty
driveway and scan the lines
of a lifetime of reading
for some kind of predictive rhythm.
She leaves Theo, who wouldn't have it
any other way. Alone is seldom
for the stay-at-home dad, seldom is
the time I have to bang my head
against the idea of my never really being alone
because thy rod and thy staff they
comfort me and just like that, yes, I feel comforted.
The words unfurl from deep childhood
programming, a code I could never live by.
Patterns of shadow and light stitch patchwork.
Give me a signal, Dad, patch me through
on a secure channel. I don't know how much longer
I can continue to listen to the white noise
of the stars, the squeal of a tile saw
across Duncan, or that one dog woofing in a hollow
place, that lone wolf in a place of echoes.

In spring, my denial still will not thaw

Tayve Neese

I walk up the mountain,
come upon skull
and ribs of a mule deer.

A purple larkspur
sprouts from its left hoof.

A thorny weed
grows from its right eye.

Foliage touches its bones
in blessing
and I wonder how it died.

I walk down the mountain,
tell myself,
I am not the bullet.
I am not the edge
of a knife.

WE ARE ALL CRUSOE IN THE SLANT LIGHT

TAYVE NEESE

of August   the pebble falls into the well

and makes no sound   the crow on the wire

loosens no feather for luck this loneliness—

a vacuum   without dust   we take

to counting   our own fingers   exponentially

we take to reading   the same James

Dickey poem each Tuesday   a single meme —

our digital connection   with no witness

of our blue-light salvation

The Lie

Connie Post

When I was in second grade
I told a girl on the playground
that I lived in the hills
surrounding our town

I told her I lived with the wild animals
and I slept under a tree each night
for decades I never understood
why I told that lie
for decades
I forgot her name

now when I think about
my father
and his shadowy exits
and entrances into my room

I think I was trying to tell her
about claws
and teeth
and the sound of growling
that comes from behind a tree

I was trying to tell her
that I understood the sound
of brush rustling
in the distance
and how a small girl
figures out
how to hide
in abandoned caves,
learns how to stay still

so not a creature
can hear her breathe

these days
I scatter blessings
and dry leaves
amongst the mourning wolves

LEARNING CLASSES

ROSE M. SMITH

Nobody told us our collars were blue
as we drifted through histories in the making
on Ohio streets, our spindly visions wrapped
in hand-me-down illusions of plenty,
our scrubbed faces made more beautiful
by grandmother-deaconess hands,
by a staunch grandfather's earned respect.

White blouses almost always—white
goes with everything, makes anything grand—
as we tapped black patents down waxed hallways
on Sundays, donned Oxfords (brown)
for treks to Shepherd Elementary School,
tops of our classes launching pads
for what was to come.

Cotillion dreams were set aside for few:
Doctors', pastors' daughters' and lawyers' sons,
the better-to-do progeny of some
whose lives moved them forward from
postal worker, forklift driver, street builder,
machinist. Coal miner heads of households
doing well enough but still an other kind,
country dust still clinging to their tall work boots.

Nobody told us that
our collars were blue, that blue remains
unless one grabs the tails of stars;
but we discerned the boundaries drawn
in privilege and place and never questioned
why the glistening edge of "more than"
seemed to move with the horizon,
one day's journey past where we had ever been.

Last Iowa Caucus

Crystal Stone

Once opened, the wine is a glassy rose
in our cups. We cheer politely
next to the dying dog. He labors
to breathe, like my own dog
the day her stomach filled
with blood like a patched and swollen moon.
The moon doesn't make it dark, my friend
tells her child when the child's eyes saucer
into planetary questions. We'd been
orbiting the food, the words, the songs.
A friend heads to the piano to play
the grief we're all avoiding. Another reads
tarot cards, tells us what we need to hear.
Outside, next to the lake, mice and rabbit
tracks are not parallel lines. I wonder
who started the chase, or if they were
friends meeting for the first time.
Will we cross over politely? The geese
and swans share the open water, the icy
beach. On the other side of the bridge,
a man corkscrews the ice open.
The splinters on the surface extend—
fingers of an open palm
waiting to be read, held.

My Phone: A Tombstone Memorializing

Crystal Stone

failed dates—mostly men
I don't remember, men I haven't wanted.
My best friend says I'm lucky
to be where I am. Today,
drinking chamomile vodka
with grapefruit. I try not to hate
myself for minutes at a time.
I haven't written a poem in two weeks
and no one's asked. What would break
my parents' hearts more: admitting I'm bi,
or disowning God? My house is empty.
I'm tired of being fat. Autocorrect changes
"cried" to "fried." I dream every night
about women. The gossiping winds
won't hush. The ants colonize
the carpet. I read the morning paper.
The bees survived the burning church.

Derek Drove the John Deere Tractor

Sharon Tracey

Derek drove the John Deere tractor
to the house this morning
to mow the small field in the side yard,
and in doing so, freed
the trunk of the old red maple
from ferns, brambles, and goldenrod.

It now rises unencumbered,

its limbs sheathed in greater lengths of lichen,
a second skin, more minted. I bend
to pick up broken ones, carry the ribs
bleached by sun to the edge
and return to hug Old Red.

Under the living branches it smells like old man.

Some things are not describable
in their humble dignity. But you can stand
with an old tree and weep,
breathe in the sour air.

After the Wildfire

Sharon Tracey

Where are the dental records for the deer,
the mountain lion, the September cubs
born in the shade of the ceanothus
in the foothills north of Los Angeles?
Where are the records for the blue-eyed
bobcat, the gray fox? The California quail
with its feathered plume who would rather
run than fly, the underbrush its palace.
When the smoldering died down, we hiked
the hills and searched for signs of life
in the riparian rubble. Scoured a path
through scorched scrub oak. Heard no growl,
no whirring wing, no chatter. The stars
went out. The wind conspired with the fire.

Rupture

Laura Van Prooyen

When the surgeon
      cuts into me, an injured starling

under the evergreen is nearly lost
      to spreading pus. Burst appendix, spray of pain.

I thought I was done with pine needles
      stuck to my knees, praying for impossible things.

The body will need to be flushed. Dead birds
      do not spring back. My hope, disproportionate.

One inch equals how much? I'm full of toxic slush.
      Abscess, pain killers, abdominal drain.

My map is a shoebox where I rest,
      tucked on a tuft of grass. Or am I'm praying again?

Around the Block

Laura Van Prooyen

I practice my inability to tell the future
and when I fail
I blame my phone.

        Short-circuit.

A child named Vincent rides his bicycle
around the block. So few children
outdoors
        anymore

        and fewer named in such a way

as to conjure wildness,
        thick-textured paint.

People now take pictures of themselves in bathrooms
    some even as they go. This

is what passes for entertainment.

Vincent doesn't know this. He doesn't
have a phone.
        No portrait mode.

Barefoot. Both ears intact.
        He pedals. Dogs bark.

Reviews

Unfinished Murder Ballads
by Darren Demaree
(Backlash Press, 2020)

Reviewed by Elizabeth Nichols

Darren Demaree's *Unfinished Murder Ballads* is timely, dark collection that serves as a meditation of the horror of the present moment. Demaree uses each word, each image to craft vignettes of the weird, the eerie, violence, and death. Readers will feel as if they opened a forbidden poetry book locked away in *The Cabin in the Woods*, or perhaps a missing section of a horror movie screenplay. And, like a critically acclaimed horror film, Demaree taps into some of humanity's greatest fears—depravity, insanity, murder—to reveal hidden truths about the poems' subjects. Great horror looks at the darkest subjects, the most morbid fantasies and twisted desires, and it looks at them unabashedly. It stares into the gross depths of things that humanity would otherwise leave alone. And, in doing so, it reveals truths that are difficult and ugly to acknowledge, but also necessary, revelatory, and cathartic—not unlike poetry itself.

The horror in Demaree's work comes quietly upon the subjects in his poems, inserting itself into sluggish mundane moments, slowly revealing its terrifying visage layer by layer. In "The Banker Took His Lunch to the Park," the banker sits in an empty park, enjoying the solitude for his afternoon respite. All is pleasant and sober. But then, an omniscient speaker reveals to the reader, "True, dark minds / don't wait for the seasons to change. For them, it's always killing season, / and when an excellent suit arrives alone, hangs itself to be inspected, the / inspector must oblige." The banker is "selected to be shreds of a body," and he never feels the flood that overtakes him. In "The Only Dedicated Cowboy in Columbus, Ohio Objects To The Price Of His Black Coffee," an AT&T communications technician moves through a routine, banal day before leaving the reader on an ominous note: "Now, though, the slack before him was demanding two dollars for a / black coffee, and that wore on him the way a bad hand would have worn on / the Duke. His father had been a tax attorney, and bequeathed him no rifle. / He would need to go the pawn shop again." In these poems, Demaree upsets expectations by lulling the reading into peaceful, normative scenes before the frightening imagery takes over. It is a classic tool in the horror genre's toolbox, but Demaree uses it to great effect, amplifying the impact with visceral imagery, repetition, and metaphor.

Other poems have an enthralling horror-movie aesthetic that dips into several sub-genres, such as slasher, psychological, monster, and even comedy horror. The poem "It Was A Question of Ownership" plays out like the climax of a horror film, introducing to the reader to a woman taking revenge on her controlling partner. With each stab of a needle into her partner's body, we learn more about the woman's relationship and her motivation for murder; physicality punctuates each flashback:

> "Even with an intimacy granted, wished for, desired, she had never wanted to be held nor hinted at belonging to him. The first needle was for his hand that never left her ass. The second needle was for him calling her ten times a night when she went out and he stayed home. The third needle was for making an enemy out of her own bed. The fourth needle was for his claim that only he would love her. The fifth needle was for ripping up her favorite sweater. The sixth needle was for ripping up her favorite picture of her wearing her favorite sweater. All of the needles were bought, paid for with his credit card, because that motherfucker became so heavy that it took his blood leaving the scene for her to feel even the smallest touch of freedom."

Psychological and comedy horror are both at play in the poem. The omniscient speaker describes how each slight against the woman builds and builds until the woman undertakes violent, methodical revenge against her partner. Demaree deftly avoids *telling* the reader the state of the woman's mind, and instead shows the reader through imagery. Dark humor appears in lines six through eight with the ripping of the woman's sweater and subsequent ripping of a picture of the same sweater. The purchase of the murder weapons with the partner's credit card underscores the woman's perception that her partner bought his own death with each incident of mistreatment. The choice to use multiple needles as murder weapons parallels the emotional needling and pain of every insult that hurt the woman. Needles also have a strong association with the feminine, conjuring images of sewing (a traditionally feminine profession or hobby) and even Sleeping Beauty pricking her finger on a the needle of a spinning wheel. The woman, then, chooses weapons that are aligned with the feminine to exact revenge on her implied misogynist partner. Demaree, in essence, skillfully condenses the run time of a one to two hour horror movie into ten lines of poetry.

Unfinished Murder Ballads, in fact, showcases Demaree's talent for telling a story in just a monostich, couplet, or tercet. "Strobe-Effect" is an excellent example. The poem is only one line long, yet carries a weight that belies its length: "If all you ever saw was the frame after the frame you wanted to see, you / would want to destroy the whole film, too." In a flash, Demaree captures a roiling frustration that begets destruction. The middle section of the collection parallels the powerful brevity of poems like "Strobe Effect." Demaree has selected six black and white images of the underbelly of towns and places forgotten. They are haunting images that elicit more questions than they can answer. These static images of a home in ruins, a dilapidated slat house left to sink into the earth, a splintering façade of a video store, and a seedy, torn 'Dead Animals' sign evoke a nameless disquietude that becomes all the more insidious for its mystery. As if contemplating the stills from a film noir, the reader is left to anxiously wrestle with the wreckage, certain that something insidious, something *wrong* has taken place. These images also feel distinctly rural and impossibly remote. As if, perhaps, they are snapshots taken of the places described in poems like "Lilac Horses," "In Some Towns There Is Only One Public Official And One Sex Worker," and "The Girl Was A Raspberry." In short, Demaree's use of the monostich and other short form poems not only beautifully align with the evocative images in the middle section, but also tie back into the larger motifs at work in the collection.

In the end, the reader does not witness any subject of these vignettes triumphing over the horror. Instead, they seem to become fully engulfed in nightmares of their own creation, or else meet sudden and often violent ends. The few that remain unscathed are still affected and changed by what they have seen, or what they have been told. The manager of the gas station in

"Lilac Horses," for example, seems compelled to the tell speaker the unsettling truth that lies beneath the field of purple flowers "growing a dozen or so yards behind the restroom outliers." The manager explains, "they used to bury horses there, when they were allowed to do such things," and that "his grandmother always told him that horseflesh gave special gifts to the flora." The speaker replies, "It feels monstrous." Now each both the manager and the speaker are privy to an uncomfortable, monstrous truth; they have a shared catharsis. And, in turn, the speaker is telling the story to the reader by way of the poem. Demaree's *Unfinished Murder Ballads*, however, is not merely about catharsis. "I / want to say the awful things that plum and dip inside my scattered, ecstatic / freedom," the speaker dilvulges to the reader in "Through The Skin of The Lip," "I don't want it to be okay. I just want to find the sharpness of my / angles of descent." The speaker, in other words, wants to understand the darkness inside of himself; he need look no further than *Unfinished Murder Ballads*.

The Unexploded Ordnance Bin
by Rebecca Foust
(Swan Scythe Press, 2018)

Reviewed by Linda E. Kim

Even before the poetry begins, Rebecca Foust's book sets the tone with a quote from Nick Flynn: "The ticking is the bomb." This is the experience of reading *The Unexploded Ordnance Bin*: every tick leads to dread with every beat bringing about a hush of anticipation. Lineation emphasizes the impact of dread, the anticipation of enjambment. Form begets meaning. Unsaid words linger. Caesura is meaningful. Suspense comes in the form of periods of finality, with commas creating moments of silence. They are held breaths of revelation, interspersed with chilling images that bloom in between ticks of silence. The absence of sound carries its own weight as subtext morphs the imagination. And all the while the poetry escalates in tensity as the speaker's anxieties churn.

To be a mother is to be held on the knife edge of fear. A child is vulnerability made flesh. Even more so when a fragile newborn is held hostage to the whims of genetic roulette:

>our son found the hollow shell
>snub-nosed & finned
>& looking like an Acme cartoon bomb
>where we raked for clams
>he wanted to keep it
>& we wanted to let him
>...
>it's too small to be seen
>the gene causing autism   but I imagine it
>anyway with snub nose & fins

The guilt and horror of passing on bad genes beleaguers her imagination. The impending discovery acts as the ticking of the bomb. Processing and internalizing this revelation is difficult enough. She's then further struck with the sheer absurdity of the thought, "needle in a haystack times ten

53

/ the chance my son would get this gene" with the sheer randomness of it worsening the guilt.

> How can a mother tend to her orchard?
> The sun continues its consort with bones
> and seeds, skin no more
> than a wet petal translucent on pavement.

In raising an autistic child, the speaker is always bracing for sudden trauma, sudden loss. And yet the child lives and "Everything Golden Is Spilled":

> You were born and your hour was silver,
> new moonlight strewn
>
> on dark ground. Pearls, seeds, wide banks
> of clouds, your bright hair,
>
> your damp, sleeping lap-weight, scalp's
> yolky chuff, tug at the nipple,
>
> the universe contracted to suck and glow;
> grain, drops of rain,
>
> dreams for a time ripening and bending
> wheat weighted with seed.

Giving birth is primal act of life. In becoming part of something greater than herself, the speaker is left overwhelmed with wonderment and awe. But that awe is torn asunder when pitted against encroaching death: "My son has chest pains again. / *I thought we were past this.*" The collapse of security, the bereavement of safety, leads to an abrupt sense of vertigo. Like ground falling away from beneath the speaker's feet. But this happens on daily basis. She is constantly forced to confront such stressors, which only bring anguish, but she must bear them time and time again.

The speaker endures even more stressors when she considers the state of the world. The world is a pressure cooker of hate, churning a toxic cocktail of racism and prejudice and the politics of fear. Borders divide. Refugees flee pointless death. Undocumented immigrants fall between the cracks of an apathetic yet hostile society. Suffering is all too easily wrought by human hands.

> Beyond the border they could smell the rain.
> It smelled like freedom. Freedom and home.
> The desert composes its requiem.
> ...
> They got lost, then they lost their water. The sun
> was a furnace blast. Dust. Thirst. Delirium,
> the desert composing its requiem.
> ...
> He made a neat stack of his clothes, and at dawn
> he lay down. He burst like a ripe sunset, a plum.

The speaker beholds the world her child will inherit and it stuns her with horror. It's a world where "human rage finally refined / into the clarity / of pure air" and this wounds her. She used to believe, "when to be human / was all promise & radiance" but she comes to realize "the world has grown old, / and I want that bud / of boy back, packed with what might / yet bloom, each spiraled sepal / still sealed, and nothing, nothing revealed."

The agony of motherhood is to wrestle with this cognitive dissonance: love is an invitation for pain. And yet the speaker cannot help it. Her child is worth it. "You: cells of my cells, blood of my blood, bone of my bone, / my flesh echo. The womb / is a semipermeable membrane, and an echo a voice that hears / what it calls."

This makes the speaker want to stand between the world and her child and embody the "...*ecclesiastical,* a prayer, / an intercessory prayer or petition. / *Intercessory*, come between. Intercede, yes—my body— / between yours—and—theirs."

In the end becoming a mother seems a paradoxical choice. It's difficult to reconcile with the fact that children cannot be entirely protected out of the womb. And yet there is beauty in fragility. And ephemeral joys are made all the more sweeter, more tender, when rooted in knowing sacrifice.

THE TASTE OF EARTH
by Hedy Habra
(Press 53, 2019)

Reviewed by Elizabeth Nichols

In Hedy Habra's *The Taste of Earth* poetry allows "the past, present and future come together at once" in a dazzling exploration of memory, human experience, and the self. Habra taps into each of the five senses in this collection, letting the reader viscerally inhabit the worlds brought to life in the poems. The poems' speaker explores a poignant, rich personal history of a halcyon childhood shattered by war, culminating in diaspora. The speaker's need to try and make sense of her experiences creates a compelling narrative that drives the collection forward. Using imagery, implied and extended metaphors, and personification, Habra masterfully captures the ineffable, at times paradoxical, human perception of time and memory. With the speaker as a guide, the reader travels through liminal, dream-like spaces that are at once ancient and modern, familiar and unfamiliar. Habra's *Taste of Earth* demonstrates that history, personal experience, and dreams are more interconnected than is realized, and it is in examining those connections that a better understanding of the self is achieved. As the speaker reveals, "It takes a lifetime to find an alphabet to weave the / shreds of images projected onto the screen of our waking mind / into a legible map that reveals our own features."

The poem "Meditations Over the Eye of Horus" is a stand-out example of Habra's poetic genius, and the themes at work in the collection. It is here that Habra puts her finger on the pulse of liminality. In the poem, Habra breaks down the Eye of Horus—an ancient Egyptian symbol also known as a Wadjet—into its six representative parts: smell, sight, thought, hearing, taste, and touch. The corresponding six sections of the poem viscerally delve into the speaker's memories by focusing on one of those senses. The speaker transports the reader into her past in Heliopolis where "creamy blossoms released their pent-up fragrance," her "father placed blessed medals in the / foundations of our home," and the "organ grinder's small / monkey danced to the tune of his red vest and tasseled fez." The poem, however, does not exist in the limited binary of the speaker's personal past and present. The very title of the poem begins an intersection of vast swaths of time, place, and human experience by using the Eye of Horus as a meditative anchor. While the focus is on the speaker's past, both ancient and present time break into the meditations, as in section 3, "Thought = 1/8:"

> "Senet, of the game of passing, led players
> through the ten regions of darkness before rising dawn, offering a glimpse of immortality. I was often on my father's lap as he faced his backgammon opponents at the Club. I still feel the throw of dice on the wooden board, sense his excitement with each pawn placed in my hand. Nefetari is portrayed playing senet solo in her sheer linen dress and gold
> bracelets. Was she conjuring fate or her inner self, bracelets clanking together with each casting of lapis and ebony sticks? Through sepia lenses, I watch my grandmother on her wheelchair, playing solitaire for hours. Was she weighing the odds of walking again, despite Lourdes and her daily Bible reading? Her ghost wrapped itself in an ink wash around my
> mother, guiding her hands as she aligned the cards, time after time."

Ancient life is transposed onto the speaker's modern past with images of Nefetari and the speaker's grandmother blurring together. Nefetari's gold bracelets are juxtaposed against the grandmother's solitaire cards, which appear again in the mother's hands. Each image of Nefetari and the grandmother is then followed by a question, supporting their similarity within the poem's structure. Moreover, the ancient game senet is echoed in the modern game of solitaire. Even the senses themselves bleed into one another, folding in upon themselves until it is impossible for the speaker to know where one begins and another ends: "Horus's lunar eye extends a hand, linking sight with / touch. The Wadjet in midst of a palm wards the evil eye. / Fatima's palm or *Khamsa* shows a finger for each of the five / senses. Can we ever separate senses?" Note, too, the use of both the past and present tense in the poem: "the game of passing **led**" and "I *watch*." At once the poem takes place in the ancient past, the immediate past, and the present with the speaker's reflective queries about Nefetari and her grandmother. Here, Habra captures a paradox at the heart of human experience: although the human conception of time is linear, the human experience of time is not. The past has an immediacy that belies the centuries, decades, days, and hours that have gone by. The speaker grapples with this paradox in the poem "After Twenty-Five Years:" "I'd pace the streets to gather some crumbs of what I / miss the most, traces of a city hidden / under my eyelids. This is not what the heart remembers, I say / to myself until the jacaranda's blue light anchors me back, / whispering, yes, it's here, deep inside…." The immediacy of the past is heightened through lush sensory experiences, imbuing the speaker's memories with a poignant emotional resonance that seems too heavy to be contained in Habra's stanzas.

Liminality, in other words, is central to The Taste of Earth. In Habra's collection, liminality (from the Latin word līmen, meaning "a threshold") is as much a transitory physical place as it is a state of the human mind. Throughout the collection, the speaker continuously crosses material, temporal, and emotional boundaries as she tries to make sense of her experiences, particularly as a member of a diasporic community. In "The Map of Memory," the speaker describes the chaotic intersection of her idyllic childhood touring damask and silk lined shops in Souk Ayass with the images of the war that came after: "bullet holes scar bronze arms, / pierce legs and chests, / speak of layers of bloodstains…." And then, "Decades later" she cannot recognize the heart of Beirut, at all. "I can no longer find / my bearings," she explains, "highways crisscross / a city once mine / in the map of memory. / A needed erasure after fifteen / years of madness, / an amnesiac reconstruction / …removing scars from facades…." Maps, faces, mirrors, roots, and screens are images that appear again and again in the collection, pointing to the speaker's attempts to understand how the chaotic and seemingly dissonant events in her life connect to one another. The times and places revisited through poetry become introspective spaces where "parallel / worlds merge on the fault line of a folded image" and the speaker endeavors to "learn / the language of invisible scars" tattooed all over her skin. The liminal state of the speaker's mind, in other words, allows her to plumb the depths of not only her memories but also her self.

Contemporary English political philosopher John Gray, discussing the conception of the inner self and consciousness, wrote that, "The inner life of humans is episodic, fuzzy, disjointed, and at times chaotic. There is no self that is more or less self-aware, only a jumble of experiences that are more or less coherent. We pass through our lives fragmented and disconnected, appearing and reappearing like ghosts…." Indeed, ghosts haunt Habra's collection, wandering in and out of poems in defiance of time and natural order: the quintessential liminal beings. The speaker visits museums with her mother's ghost by her side, and her grandmother's ghost wraps "itself in an ink wash" around her mother. Even when figures are not literally described as ghosts, they appear as silhouettes, "gliding as faceless pawns," or only as detached echoes and voices. In "Vanishing Point," the speaker passes dream-like through another liminal space: a street where young men "recede and peel off the / murals, disintegrate like antique parchments…." In *The Taste of Earth*, there is a consistent theme of trying to gather fragmented memories into a cohesive whole—of deciphering phantasmagoria to find meaning in chaos.

Fittingly, the collection does not come to a neat conclusion. In the final poem an old, abandoned fountain is personified. Once again, the image of a mirror appears; this time, in a simile: "I hear voices, fractured like shattered mirrors, each searching / for an ear, unable to find a match, lost cries soar in dissonance…" The fountain describes feeling broken and forgotten, unable to soothe children's wounded feet because its well is empty. Much like the speaker and her fragmented memories, the fountain has only rubbles and the discordant voices of the past to draw upon to try and understand itself. In the end, there is a return to a place that is now unrecognizable from the cool, water-filled marble fountain of the past. This return is reminiscent of the fable *The History of Rasselas, Prince of Abyssinia*, written by eighteenth century English Writer and philosopher Samuel Johnson. In it, Prince Rasselas leaves his home, "the Happy Valley" to travel to other countries. But, he becomes bored and unhappy in his travels. Moreover, everyone he meets in the outside world throughout his travels is also unhappy. Ultimately, Rasselas gives up his search for happiness, and returns to his home in "the Happy valley." Yet, despite his return, Rasselas is still unhappy. As Johnson reveals in the final act of his fable, neither Rasselas nor "the Happy valley" can ever be what they were when he left. The prince's effort to reclaim the happiness of the past is an impossible endeavor. Habra inadvertently captures Rasselas' experience as he returns to "the Happy valley," the prince and the speaker's voices echoing each other in the poem "The House of Happiness:"

> "I wanted to revisit the house of happiness
> and found open doors and windows
> a house where anyone can enter and I can't step out
>
> I tried to dive into the swelling well of memories
> slide between yellowed images
> sample once more the bittersweet taste of farewell
>
> I used to walk by jasmine hedges redolent
> of passerby thread white buds
> rolled around my wrists rippling over my chest
>
> I wished to retrace forgotten steps steeped in oleander
> but only see dried-up vines deserted
> sidewalks where shadows sink in their own reflections."

The speaker's "search / for new equations / to rebuild [her] notions / of belonging, memory or desire" has not brought back the exact happiness she once felt. The fountain can never be as sparklingly resplendent as it once was. But, as Habra proves in *The Taste of Earth*, poetry "conjures a face, each faded, a / glance, a touch, even shattered words bring eroded memories / to life." The reconstruction and reexamination of the past through poetry engenders a deeper understanding of the present, and of the self. The speaker's journey in *The Taste of Earth* is valuable because it honors the human experience.

Frances of the Wider Field
by Laura Van Prooyen
(Lily Poetry Review Books, 2021)

Reviewed by Amy Strauss Friedman

What do we mean when we say we should just be ourselves? No person is an island; we are amalgamations of our own muddied memories and those of others, composites of our agendas and theirs. Laura Van Prooyen's new book of poetry *Frances of the Wider Field* questions the value and impediments of memory and nostalgia, and if it is even possible to see ourselves clearly at all. Her poems are a recognition of these complexities, these endless questions, this preservation of the past through today's struggles.

The molding of memory into nostalgia proves that flashbacks are never just facts. Rather, they are first-person narrations, which are by their very nature unreliable. After we dress them in new clothes, the ones we would choose to wear rather than the inherited wardrobe of the last designer, we become a link in the chain of inherited memory that develops into an endless game of generational telephone. Our ancestors become an assemblage of contextualized memory, and caricatures of who they really were. For who is anyone without the gaze of another to recognize them? And who are we without the stories we tell ourselves?

We struggle to simultaneously remember accurately those we've loved and lost, so as to hold ourselves to some level of factual truth amidst our jagged emotional responses, and to integrate our memories of loved ones into our own stories. In this way, we come to learn that all memory is projection, a push/pull that demands we speak, and yet that we stay silent for fear of misrepresentation. Stories must pass on, and yet since they will never adhere to strict rules of realism, they push against our desire to tell them. In the narrator's recognition of this impossibility, her mother becomes "Frances of all things and of no things." What does the narrator mean when she mentions Frances? "When I say Frances, I mean a woman. I mean //a place. The dead cling to the land. The living cling /to a story that, like currency, changes hands." She leaves open the possibility of misinterpreting Frances, of not limiting her to one story when Frances was/is so much larger than that. "Even without a body, you're both //cataract and sight," the author tells Frances, cognizant that what appears clear also appears cloudy, and the impossibility of determining which, if either, are authentic.

Without categorical answers, the reader wonders if memory nudges us to live in the past instead of finding joy in the present. And yet, we also wonder if we can find joy without remembrance. The struggle to answer these questions collapses time and memory, layer upon layer. "I'm going backwards. A century of muscle /grips my bones," Van Prooyen insists. The present pulls us backward; the past propels us forward. The world telescopes into itself. "My whole childhood could fit on the tip /of a lit cigarette," we are told in the poem "Flood."

Overlaying past on present creates a new present, one more stratified and complex and worth having. At times the reader struggles to tell who's who in this book or how they are intertwined, and this is exactly the point. The narrator is and is not Frances, is and is not Jenny, is and is not her father, her brother, others. Disentangling ourselves from people and allegories that have shaped us is, mercifully, impossible. Our stories consist largely of other people. Van Prooyen suggests that we should never wish for an unraveling. Before the narrator is born she "was not there. I was light //if I was anything at all." Light that guided Frances, and protected her daughter. Later, the narrator "drink[s] for the girl /who, if there's mercy /never knew what was coming." She feels for herself who is made of others, and others who are made partially of her.

And Frances' memory, so much like our own, settles and wraps around her needs: "after years of telling and retelling, //my mother sees what she can bear." Frances erases the memory of the doctors who knocked her out while giving birth to her son: "She woke to find bruises all over //her baby's head," the poem "The Calumet Region" tells us. The ugly part doesn't serve Frances, so it's tossed aside. The happy parts of her son's birth then expand; they umbrella the experience. The result is that trauma does not define the narrative. And so, it also does not define the narratives of subsequent generations. "I know this,/because it's the story she told," the narrator notes of Frances, while also sharing the blessings of this endless cycle: "One daughter will say goodnight /to another daughter, her voice carrying //the future down the hall."

"Mother, I float to your ceiling, drift over //your body. Your body my heart once beat in,/where as a dark cluster of cells I began furiously to split." Mother and daughter find themselves bound up in the same life, the same body. Frances is reborn after death, and continues to morph throughout the generations. She goes from finite to infinite possibilities. For there's no escaping history/ancestry/generational inheritance of joy and pain. "How vain //to think distance might change the lines on my palm /or the chapter and verse lodged under //my tongue." But there's always the opportunity to reshape these lines, this inheritance. Van Prooyen deftly proves that this is the work of our lives.

A Piece of Peace: Everyday Mindfulness to Improve your Well-being and Creativity.
by Sweta Vikram

Reviewed by Ami Kaye

Side-stepping the daily bombardment of information, Sweta Vikram's new non-fiction offering—part journal-memoir, part self-help book—is based on a culmination of the author's year-long journaling after enduring a near-death experience. *A Piece of Peace* digests, organizes, and delivers pertinent information in accessible and engaging bites.

The author shares her newfound wisdom after emerging from a chronic illness, touching upon the physical, emotional, and spiritual aspects of coping with the loss of control over one's life, and uses the knowledge she has gleaned through pain and suffering in order to guide readers through their own challenges. The author, who made notes on her phone from her hospital bed, touts the benefits of journaling. She draws on her transformative journey, providing a road map to inner peace and well-being by demystifying some of the complexities of our current world and lives.

She writes of the juxtaposition of East-West beliefs and traditions, the ephemeral nature of life, and living fully in the moment: "How often we take our lives for granted. Thank you, Life, for reminding me of the smallest ways in which we can experience a miracle." She goes on to reassure the reader that "Light is on the other side of your scars." Vikram writes passionately about the importance of gratitude; the beauty of silence; practical concerns such as emotional well-being, finances, and professional life; maintaining physical health; the benefits of meditation and yoga; and establishing boundaries for self-care, but also stressing the importance of compassion and gratitude: "Gratitude is the balm we need right now."

An accomplished poet and writer, Vikram understands "For writers and artists, self-care matters on a whole different and deeper level," and offers helpful tips, such as overcoming writer's block.

As we navigate the fallout from the "me-too" era, Vikram strongly advocates the need for women to step up and "stop relying on people to build you up. Stop giving away your power. Instead of seeking outside validation and approval, focus on staying authentic and building your own path."

She emphasizes that even when confronted by circumstances we cannot control, we have the tools to respond in ways that promote physical and spiritual healing, and mitigate despair. "Learn to fall in love with imperfections" says the author, advising readers to conserve their emotional energy, and focus on being kind to one's self in order to balance life and improve relationships.

The author stresses the importance of self-care, a timely reminder for those of us worn out by the "barrenness of a busy life." Vikram urges readers to maintain a positive attitude even in face of incredible challenges, and her personal narratives encourage deeper reflection from the reader.

Sweta Vikram's *A Piece of Peace* is profoundly inspiring, a beautiful articulation of courage and strength in face of impossible circumstances. The authenticity, grace, and honesty of this work will set free the elusive spark of motivation for people in search of self-empowerment.

Prompts

Jeffrey Alfier

Poems with a strong sense of Place, where Place is integral to the poem's existence, providing immediacy to the reader; "geography wedded to its people," as CD Wright put it.

Clara Burghelea

Write a poem about your name, from meaning/origin to using the senses to describe it (color, taste, smell, touch, any sound related to it). Think of it as a whimsical creature that embodies all that is visible and whatever haunts it.

Roxana Cazan

The pantoum is a Malay form of poetry imitated in the Western cultures. Like the villanelle, it consists of lines that repeat, but it is composed of quatrains. The repetition scheme asks for the following: the 2nd and 4th lines of each stanza become the 1st and 3rd of the following. Fixed form helps put order into things. Because we have been experiencing the rule of chaos recently throughout the world—Covid19—, write a pantoum that explores your life during the pandemic.

David Capps

Write a poem about your socks. But try to make it only about your socks.

Jaewon Chang

Write about an experience that you had during the coronavirus crisis (loss of family member, boredom, isolation, depression, etc.). Create a poem where you only describe the sounds of your surroundings during the experience.

Karen Douglass

"Notice daily actions and objects."

Joyce Futa

I dive into a new ocean....

Shanta Gander

Mythmaking. If you were to think of the range of fairy tales that spoke to you from your childhood, or myths that always grabbed you, how would you do your own re-imagining? For example, are there ways that you have followed breadcrumbs like Hansel & Gretel? Are you someone who has been taken by a Robber Bridegroom? Write a piece in prose, a lyric essay, or poem using the prompt.

Marina Kazakova

Where "time is coming out of water",
I'm slowly learning the rhythm
of this little stretch of aqua,
of the eyes and the palms
that inhabit this vacuum - my Venezia -
their language seems to predate all
that I've known...

Kate LaDew

There's an elephant on the interstate. Why?

Rustin Larson

Take a brief walk around your house, apartment building, or other structure. Write down everything you see that begins with the letter "J." Arrange these words in your notebook as end words of a line. Now invent the lines, writing into the words you collected.

Joseph Mills

I long ago realized that asking people what they do or where they are from usually doesn't result in very interesting information or conversations. Worse, we tend to then slot people into stereotypes. But if you say "Tell me about the accident," you'll get a specific, unexpected, story. We've all been in one in some form. This also works as a writing prompt: "Tell about the accident." And a variation, "tell about the scar."

Michael Minassian

Write a poem about an encounter you have in real life with a fictional character (for example: Madame Bovary, Holden Caulfield, Ishmael, Holly Golightly, Lisbeth Salander)

Cameron Morse

I recently wrote a poem that started with a statement. Then I wrote, "I don't know where I'm going / with this." Try that. Include your own stumble, your own moment of uncertainty in the poem. Make a statement, then negate it, take it back by saying something like, "Or maybe that's not it. That's not what happened at all," etc. Cast doubt on a favorite quote, or deconstruct an idiom. Consider ways of exercising Keat's negative capability.

Compose a poem composed entirely of poem prompts.

Tayve Neese

Think of a word related to technology or science. Pair this with a word that has a significant religious or spiritual connotation (evolution psalms/ blue-light salvation) and use this combination in the title, first line, or last line of your poem.

Connie Post

When was the last time you counted the number of days until something arrived (an event, an item, a person). Describe the waiting and what happened when it finally arrived.

Rose M. Smith

Think of an unusual license plate you've seen or a combination of letters on one or more license plates. Think of phrases beginning with those letters. Let that word or phrase be the seed for a poem.

Sharon Tracey

Open a favorite book to a random page. Select one sentence you are fond of. Write a poem to this sentence.

Laura Van Prooyen

Write a poem by creating sound associations before you consider meaning. Play with consonance, assonance, alliteration, lexical repetition, and rhyme, using sound associations as the thread that energizes your draft. Play! If you are stuck as to where to begin, randomly select a line from one of your favorite poems and start your sound riff.

CONTRIBUTOR NOTES

Jeffrey Alfier's most recent book *The Shadow Field*, was published by Louisiana Literature Journal & Press (2020). His lit journal credits include *The Carolina Quarterly, Copper Nickel, Emerson Review, Hotel Amerika, James Dickey Review, Permafrost, Vassar Review*. He is co-editor of Blue Horse Press and *San Pedro River Review*.

Clara Burghelea is a Romanian-born poet with an MFA in Poetry from Adelphi University. Recipient of the Robert Muroff Poetry Award, her poems and translations appeared in *Ambit, Waxwing, The Cortland Review* and elsewhere. Her collection *The Flavor of The Other* was published in 2020 with Dos Madres Press. She is the Review Editor of *Ezra, An Online Journal of Translation*.

A Romanian immigrant to the US, **Roxana Cazan's** work has most recently been featured in *Poets Reading the News, Flashes, Switchgrass Poetry Review, Connecticut River Review, Construction Magazine, Cold Creek Review, Hektoen International, Watershed Review, The Peeking Cat Anthology, The Portland Review, The Woody Guthrie Anthology* (Village Book Press 2019), and others. Roxana is the author of a poetry book entitled *The Accident of Birth* (Main Street Rag in 2017) and the co-editor of *Voices on the Move: An Anthology by and about Refugees* (Solis Press, 2020). She lives in Oklahoma City, where she is working on a manuscript that explores women's experiences during the COVID-19 lockdown.

David Capps is a philosophy professor at Western Connecticut State University. He is the author of three chapbooks: *Poems from the First Voyage* (The Nasiona Press, 2019), *A Non-Grecian Non-Urn* (Yavanika Press, 2019), and Colossi (Kelsay Books, 2020). His manuscript, *Drawn in Evening Light*, was a finalist for the 2020 Gasher first book scholarship. He lives in New Haven, CT.

Jaewon Chang is a high school junior living in the Philippines. His works of poetry have been recognized by literary journals, such as Cleaver Magazine, District Lit, Blue Marble Review, and more. His lifetime goal is to travel the city on foot.

Karen Douglass, BS, MA, MFA, a native New Englander, now lives in Colorado. She has been a psychiatric nurse, horsewoman, racetrack judge, mother (still is), college instructor, poet, and novelist.

Joyce Futa now lives in beautiful Altadena, California after spending 50 years of her adult life in beloved San Francisco. In both places, she found a wonderful community of writers. Her book of poetry *Lit Windows: A Book of Haibun and Tanka Prose* was published by Blue Light Press in 2017.

Shanta Lee Gander is an artist and multi-faceted professional. As an artist, her endeavors include writing and photography with written work that has been featured in *PRISM, ITERANT Literary Magazine, Palette Poetry, BLAVITY, DAME Magazine, The Crisis Magazine, Rebelle Society,* on the *Ms. Magazine Blog,* and on a former radio segment *Ponder This.* Shanta Lee's photojournalism has been featured on Vermont Public Radio (VPR.org) and her investigative reporting has been in *The Commons* weekly newspaper covering Windham County, VT. Shanta Lee is the 2020 recipient of the Arthur Williams Award for Meritorious Service to the Arts and 2020 and named as Diode Editions full-length book contest winner for her debut poetry compilation, *GHETTOCLAUSTROPHOBIA: Dreamin of Mama While Trying to Speak in Woke Tongues.* Her contributing work on an investigative journalism piece for The Commons received a New England Newspaper & Press Association (NENPA) 2019 award. Shanta Lee gives lectures on the life of Lucy Terry Prince, considered the first known African American poet in English literature, as a member of the Vermont Humanities Council Speakers Bureau and is the 2020 gubernatorial appointee to their board of directors.

Shanta Lee is an MFA candidate in Creative Non-Fiction and Poetry at the Vermont College of Fine Arts. She has an MBA from the University of Hartford and an undergraduate degree in Women, Gender and Sexuality from Trinity College. Currently, Shanta Lee Gander offers virtual creativepreneurship workshops to writers and other artists connecting them to strategies around project planning, grant writing, and other topics as a part of her Obsidian Arts, L3C .

Marina Kazakova (b. Gorky, Russia, 1983) is a Russian-born Belgium-based poet. Her literature works deal to a large degree with confrontation with the past and explore the challenges posed both by memory and grief. Published internationally in magazines and journals (Three Rooms Press "Maintenant", "Great Weather for Media...", "Crannog", "Duck Lake Books", "Writing in a Woman's Voice", "Modern Literature"), Marina is a frequent performer, she has been shortlisted at various international poetry festivals and art events: Brussels Poetry Festival 2017-2018, Maintenant's Dada London Invasion 2018, Nothing To Sell 2019 - Rome, European Poetry Festival 2020, Red Square Festival 2020, The 3rd International Literary Festival Words of Fire 2020 in Portugal, Gerard Manley Hopkins International Literary Festival 2020 in Ireland, Stanza Scotland's Poetry Festival 2021, Mani Lit Fest 2021, etc.

Marina holds Master's degrees in Public Relations and Transmedia. Currently, she is Communications Officer at Victim Support Europe (Brussels) and working on her practice-based PhD in Arts at Luca School of Arts (KULeuven).

Kate LaDew is a graduate from the University of North Carolina at Greensboro with a BA in Studio Arts. She lives in Graham, NC with her cats Charlie Chaplin and Janis Joplin.

Rustin Larson's poetry has appeared in *The New Yorker, The Iowa Review,* and *North American Review*. He won 1st Editor's Prize from *Rhino* and was a prize winner in The National Poet Hunt and The Chester H. Jones Foundation contests. A graduate of the Vermont College MFA in Writing, Larson was an Iowa Poet at The Des Moines National Poetry Festival, and a featured poet at the Poetry at Round Top Festival. He is a poetry professor at Maharishi University, a writing instructor at Kirkwood Community College, and has also been a writing instructor at Indian Hills Community College. Among his published books are *Library Rain* (Conestoga Zen Press, 2019) which was named a February 2019 Exemplar by Grace Cavalieri and reviewed in *The Washington Independent Review of Books*; *Howling Enigma* (Conestoga Zen Press, 2018); *Pavement* (Blue Light Press, 2017); *The Philosopher Savant* (Glass Lyre Press, 2015); *Bum Cantos, Winter Jazz, & The Collected Discography of Morning* (Blue Light Press, 2013); *The Wine-Dark House* (Blue Light Press, 2009); and *Crazy Star* (Loess Hills Books, 2005).

A faculty member at the University of North Carolina School of the Arts, **Joseph Mills** has published six volumes of poetry and one of fiction. His seventh collection, *Bodies in Motion,* which features poems about dance, is scheduled for publication in 2022.

Michael Minassian is a Contributing Editor for Verse-Virtual. His chapbooks include poetry: *The Arboriculturist* and photography: *Around the Bend*. Both of his poetry collections Time is Not a River and Morning Calm were published in 2020. Michael's poetry manuscript *A Matter of Timing* won the 2020 Poetry Society of Texas' Catherine Case Lubbe Manuscript Contest (publication: Summer

2021). For more information: http://michaelminassian.com

Cameron Morse is Senior Reviews editor at *Harbor Review,* a poetry editor at Harbor Editions, and the author of six collections of poetry. His first, *Fall Risk*, won Glass Lyre Press's 2018 Best Book Award. His latest is *Far Other* (Woodley Press, 2020). He holds and MFA from the University of Kansas City—Missouri and lives in Independence, Missouri, with his wife Lili and two children. For more information, check out his Facebook page or website.

Tayve Neese's work has appeared in journals and anthologies around the United States and abroad including *The Paris Review* (online edition), *Comstock Review*, *Fourteen Hills,* and *diode*. She was longlisted for the 2019 University of Canberra Vice Chancellor's International Poetry Prize in Australia. Her full-length collection of poems, *Blood to Fruit,* was published in 2015. *Locust*, her second collection of poems, is forthcoming from Salmon Poetry. She is Co-founder and Co-executive Editor of Trio House Press and Primary Editor of *The Banyan Review*, an international, online journal. Neese currently resides on a barrier island off the coast of Florida.

Connie Post served as first Poet Laureate of Livermore, California Her work has appeared in *Calyx, Comstock Review, One, Cold Mountain Review, Slipstream, Spillway, River Styx, Spoon River Poetry Review, Valparaiso Poetry Review* and *Verse Daily*. Her first full length Book *Floodwater* (Glass Lyre Press) won the 2014 Lyrebird Award. Her poetry awards include the Caesarea Award, the Liakoura Award and the Crab Creek Poetry Award. Her newest book *Prime Meridian* was released in January 2020 and was a finalist in the 2020 Best Book Awards.

Rose M. Smith lives in Central Ohio near a short stretch of woods . Her work has appeared in *Blood and Thunder, Origins Journal, Passager, The Examined Life, Snapdragon,* and other journals and anthologies. She is author of four chapbooks, most recently *Holes in My Teeth* (Kattywompus Press, 2016) and one full-length collection, *Unearthing Ida* (Glass Lyre Press, 2019), which won the 2018 Lyrebird Prize. She is an Editor with *Pudding Magazine*, a Pushcart Prize nominee, and a Cave Canem fellow.

Crystal Stone is the author of four collections of poetry: *Knock-Off Monarch* (Dawn Valley 2018), *All the Places I Wish I Died* (CLASH 2021), *Gym Bras* (Really Serious Literature 2021), and *Civic Duty* (Vegetarian Alcoholic 2022). She received her MFA in Creative Writing and Environment from Iowa State University, where she also gave a TEDx talk entitled "The Transformative Power of Poetry." You can find her on instagram at @justlikeastone and at her website www.crystalbstone.com.

Sharon Tracey is the author of *Chroma: Five Centuries of Women Artists* (Shanti Arts, 2020) and *What I Remember Most is Everything* (All Caps Publishing). In *Chroma*, the poet guides the reader through a series of galleries inspired by the work of women artists, exploring what it means to be human, a woman, a creator. Her poems have appeared in *Terrain.org, The Worcester Review, Mom Egg Review, SWWIM, The Ekphrastic Review,* and elsewhere. sharontracey.com

Laura Van Prooyen is author of three collections of poetry: *Frances of the Wider Field* (Lily Poetry Review Books)*, Our House Was on Fire* (Ashland Poetry Press) nominated by Philip Levine and winner of the McGovern Prize, and *Inkblot and Altar* (Pecan Grove Press). She is also co-author with Gretchen Bernabei of *Text Structures from Poetry*, a book of writing lessons for educators of grades 4-12 (Corwin Literacy). Van Prooyen is the Managing Editor for *The Cortland Review*, she teaches in the low-residency MFA Creative Writing program at Miami University and is the founder of Next Page Press: www.nextpage-press.com. She lives in San Antonio, TX. www.lauravanprooyen.com

Glass Lyre Press

exceptional works to replenish the spirit

Glass Lyre Press is an independent literary publisher interested in technically accomplished, stylistically distinct, and original work. Glass Lyre seeks diverse writers that possess a dynamic aesthetic and an ability to emotionally and intellectually engage a wide audience of readers.

Glass Lyre's vision is to connect the world through language and art. We hope to expand the scope of poetry and short fiction for the general reader through exceptionally well-written books, which evoke emotion, provide insight, and resonate with the human spirit.

Poetry Collections
Poetry Chapbooks
Select Short & Flash Fiction
Anthologies

www.GlassLyrePress.com

www.ingramcontent.com/pod-product-compliance
Lightning Source LLC
Chambersburg PA
CBHW030159100526
44592CB00009B/363